Wilderness

EXPLORED

Photography by GERRY ELLIS
Essays by KAREN KANE

NORTHWORD PRESS
Minnetonka, Minnesota

Introduction

IN THE COURSE OF COMPILING and photographing this book, we traveled across thousands of miles of wilderness and plowed through thousands of volumes of words—words written by the long line of strangers that came and saw and recorded.

The New World offered both intrigue and mystique to those first explorers and naturalists. They traveled still waters and wild rapids pushing farther and farther westward, sailing up coastlines and along boundary waters. Few were professional naturalists and fewer still literary scholars of the land. Often their words were roughly hewn, other times simple and straightforward, but always, they were sincere and heartfelt expressions.

From the writings, it's obvious that each individual had been caught by at least a single moment when the breadth of this wilderness took them by surprise—the same surprise that even today greets those who step to the edge of the viewing platform of the Grand Canyon or see their first wild killer whale under the cry of a soaring bald eagle.

Wilderness continues to inspire the human spirit, and even now, gives that spirit breathing room.

Now, as we offer you this rich glimpse of an early America, we'd like to share with you a quote by naturalist Edward Abbey that we thought of often while putting this book together:

"I am not a naturalist; what I hope to evoke through words here is the way things feel on stormy desert afternoons, the exact shade of color in shadows on the warm rock, the brightness of October . . . and a few other simple, ordinary, inexplicable things like that."

Gerry Ellis
Karen Kane

Southeast
Wilderness

THIS AREA that became the threshold of the new world offered both intrigue and mystique to the first explorers and naturalists. For the Southeast is a land of very differing perspectives and profound extremes.

Exotic islands that echo with the screech of wild parrots. Damp, misty rain forests a thousand shades of emerald. Coral reefs and turquoise water baking in soft, hot sun. A paradise.

Then inland swamps of palpable humidity, singing with the sounds of insects that either bite or sting. Water moccasins moving sluggishly in brackish water, monstrous alligators that lay in wait in the primordial muck. Hostility.

A hundred miles away sweet gum trees mix with cherry and birch, American hornbeam and elm. Cool green forests climb the misty slopes of the blue-ridged mountains. Warm summer sunlight filters through leaves to a chorus of songbirds. Black bear and cougar and wolves move about like forest phantoms; squirrels chatter in the treetops. A refuge, quiet and refreshing.

It goes on—barrier islands and rain forests, broad, lazy rivers and shifting dunes.

Imagine the wonder and amazement of the first explorers as they innocently opened up the last continent to the world, stepping first into a region that would both embrace and reject, awe and terrify over and over again. One by one, the secrets were uncovered. Secrets, that for the most part, remain intact today.

*And therefore I followed its coast eastwards for one hundred and
seven leagues to the point where it ended. And from that cape, I saw
another island, distant eighteen leagues from the former, to the east, to
which I at once gave the name "Espanola." And I went there and followed its northern coast, as I had in the case of Juana, to the eastward for one hundred and eighty-eight great leagues in a straight line.
This island and all the others are very fertile to a limitless degree, and
this island is extremely so. In it there are many harbors on the coast
of the sea, beyond comparison with others which I know in
Christendom, and many rivers, good and large, which is marvelous.
Its lands are high, and there are in it very many sierras and very
lofty mountains, beyond comparison with the island of Tenerife.
All are most beautiful, of a thousand shapes, and all are accessible.
Espanola is a marvel.*

The First Letter of Columbus, 1490s

Fowles also there be many, both upon land and upon sea: but concerning them on land I am not able to name them, because my abode was there so short. But for the fowle of the fresh rivers, these two I noted to be the chiefe, where of the Flemengo is one, having all red feathers, and long red legs like a herne, a necke according to the bill, red, whereof the upper neb hangeth an inch over the nether: and egript, which is all white as the swanne, with legs like to an hearnshaw, and of bignesse accordingly, but it hath in her taile feathers of so fine a plume, that it passeth the estridge his feather.

Of the sea-fowle above all other not common in England, I noted the pellicane, which is fained to be the lovingst bird that is; which rather than her young should want, wil spare her heart bloud out of her belly; but for all this lovingnesse she is very deformed to beholde.

Sir John Hawkins, 1560s
English Naval Commander

Atlantic & Eastern Forests
Wilderness

RIVULETS OF AIR, gentle and unexpected this late in the summer, undulate across an open sea of sedge grass. A sweet perfume of drying grass and autumn rides the invisible current eastward over the colonnade of pines and transient sand dunes and out to sea.

In spring, when the eastern forests are in bloom, it is the fragrance of swamp cedar, cypress, palm, laurel, magnolia, evergreen, a variety of hardwoods, and a myriad of flowering shrubs that drifts for miles.

It has been this way for centuries—winds carrying the aroma of the inland forests over the shifting dunes and out to sea. Early explorers were mesmerized by the fragrance of these unknown forests.

In summer, the forest was a continuous wave of green, soaking moisture from a warm, humid blanket of air that covered the land. A single valley sometimes held more than seventy species of trees. Eastern red squirrels chattered their agitated warning to passers-by from the boughs of evergreens, black bears raised their young among the blackberry brambles and mountain lions haunted the valleys. The woodlands rejoiced in the melodies of warblers, fly-catchers, thrushes and jays.

But perhaps for those first explorers the shining moment for the eastern forests was autumn. As days began to shorten and each dawn extended frost a few miles farther south, a wash of autumnal tints—terra-cotta, cranberry, pumpkin, and honey-yellow—transformed the eastern forests into a natural spectacle unlike any other on earth.

A flocke of cranes, the most white, arouse by us, with such a cry as if an Army of men had shouted together . . . goodly-tall Cedars . . . of excellent smell and qualitie . . . about 14 severall sorts of sweete smelling tymber trees. The highest and reddest Cedars of the world, bettering those of the Assores, Indies or [Lebanon].

Phillip Amidas and Arthur Barlow, 1584
English Navigators

[In fall, the wild geese] afterwards proceed southward, with great cries, and hopping along with an almost incredible swiftness; at the same time there came also swans, cranes, heron, ducks and various other kinds of birds and fowls.

Deleware Indians to Early Settlers

What I saw every day and in the greatest numbers was trees . . .
It is not only continual forest, but a very monotonous forest, there
being little variety . . . In the eternal woods it is impossible to keep off
a particularly unpleasant, anxious feeling, which is excited irrestibly by
the continuing shadow and the confined outlook.

Dr. J. D. Schoeph, Late 1700s
Surgeon

Before the arrival of the Europeans, the whole country was a Wood,
The Swamps full of Cripple & Brush; and the Ground unbroke . . .
[The land] is varied with pleasant, swelling knobs, brooks and little
lakes. In its vegetation it abounds with sweet-maples, linden, birch,
elm, white pines in some places; and with goose-berry underwoods on
the north side of all the ridges.

Lewis Evans, Circa 1745
Geographer

North & Northeast
Wilderness

THERE IS AN IDENTITY to the landscape in the far north that is defined by color. White. Blue. Gray. The colors of the land, the water and the sky. Snow. Ocean. Ice.

The animals add little color variation. Polar bears. Beluga whales. Snowy owls. Harp seals. All white. Superbly adapted to their environment, the animals of the far north live simply within the forces of nature that shape their home. The vast icescape of the far north forces simplicity.

The land also forces singleness of purpose. To those who were unfamiliar with its demands, the far north was a raging, frozen hell. Enormous seas, frigid cold, crushing pack ice, sweeping winds, frostbite, and starvation were the forces to conquer. Or to simply survive.

The forests in the north also presented simplicity and singularity. Like a giant ocean, the tree cover created an endless monotony not unlike the desolation of the Arctic.

Explorers complained bitterly about the dark forest, and its rocky or swampy underlayment. Both presented difficult obstacles to traverse. Mile after mile, explorers and settlers slowly hacked their way through a forest so full and so thick that the sun could hardly penetrate.

Today, we can count ourselves fortunate that evergreens, hardwoods, and flowering shrubs still form a great forest that blankets the east with a sea of green as pure and intense as the shades of white in the Arctic Ocean.

This river begins just beyond the island of Assumption, opposite to the high mountains of Honguedo, and the width across is some thirty-five or forth leagues, with a depth in the middle of 200 fathoms. The whole country on both sides of this river. . . is as fine a land and as level as ever one beheld. There are some mountains visible at a considerable distance from the river, and into it several tributaries flow down from these. This land is everywhere covered and overrun with timber of several sorts and also with quantities of vines. . . There are a large number of big stags, does, bears and other animals.

We beheld the footprints of a beast with but two legs, and followed his tracks over the sand and mud for along distance. Its paws were more than a palm in size. Furthermore there are many otters beavers, martens, foxes, wild-cats, hares, rabbits, squirrels, wonderfully large [musk]rats and other wild beasts. . . You will meet with many whales, porpoises, sea-horses and Adhothuys, which is a species of fish that we had never seen or heard of before.

They are as white as snow and have a head like a greyhound's. Their habitat is between the ocean and the freshwater that begins between the river Saguenay and Canada.

Jacques Cartier, 1535
Explorer

. . . . is very beautiful and attractive. Along the bank it seemed as
if the trees had been planted there in most places for pleasure. . .
here are many cranes, as white as swans. . . a forest of firs, which are
the common resort of partridges and rabbits. . . a very beautiful and
agreeable country crossed by several little brooks and two small rivers
which empty into this lake; and a great many ponds and meadows,
where there were an unlimited amount of game, many vines, and
beautiful woods, and a great number of chestnut trees, of which the
fruit was still in the burr.

Samuel de Champlain, 1613
Discoverer

The fog through which we had hitherto been sailing, scaled off at this moment, disclosing to our gaze one of the grandest sights that we ever beheld, for directly in front of us, rose a huge, rocky bastion, the precipitous sides of which were occupied by myriads of Awks, Guillemots, and Puffins, thousands of snowy plumaged Gannets floated in the air over the high clifts, while the water below was thickly dotted with various species. . . Among the most noticeable birds on the rock, were the Gannets, and they occupied a considerable space on the north-west side of the upper portion. Here . . . the. . . bulky nests which were composed of seaweed, were placed in long rows, about a foot apart, reminding one strongly of hills of corn. . . Early in the morning, when all the birds were on the nests, they presented a singular appearance, for there was fully a quarter of an acre of Gannets. . . and when we reached the edge of the precipice, there were, at least, ten thousand Gannets before us, flying high over the surging waves. A sight like this. . . strongly reminded one of a snow-storm, when the countless flakes whirl in wild confusion.

C. J. Maynard, 1881
Author

Central & Grasslands
Wilderness

MORNING on the unending panorama that is the grasslands of America has a soft persuasion about it that makes one feel as though they were born here, and should never venture from the spot. Long, thin, fawn-colored shafts of grass, mute in the lightless dawn, their tips feathered in sheathed seed heads, dance in light breezes.

The wind softly delivers the meadowlark's message, the greetings of a cricket. Bison, grazing in a saddle of gently dipping golden ground, lift their heads to flare black nostrils at its touch. The wind carries with it the breath of the earth—flower-scented in spring, sun-baked in summer, parched in fall, frost-stiffened in winter.

To those who first lived upon or crossed the prairie on foot, this rolling land seemed an endless Eden. Hundreds of thousands of bison and large herds of elk, deer, and pronghorn once called the prairie home, as well as millions of migrating waterfowl, including most of the world's sandhill cranes, and the now-rare whooping crane.

To the north, the soft grasslands yield to an opposite extreme. Rough and caustic, the "bad lands," as they were termed by the first explorers, offer only eroded, dry, lifeless, and seasonally extreme expanses of ancient rock. It is a stark contrast of life and scale.

Banded with colors of earthly hues, the buttes and cliffs of the Badlands echo the deposits of sediment that settled millions of years ago. The Badlands are a testament to a land sculpted by the elements. The very austerity of the place is its beauty.

The American Bison has for a long period been the ruling power of the plains. Its vast herds have been the wonder of visitors.

Though yet seen in considerable numbers in some localities, there is a monstrous sacrifice of the creatures steadily going on; and some time in the near future they will be reduced to the condition of their allies in Europe.

Audubon says: "In the days of our boyhood and youth, Bison roamed over the small and beautiful prairies of Indiana and Illinois. Herds of them stalked through the woods on Kentucky and Tennessee; but they had dwindled down to a few stragglers, which resorted to the barrens, towards the year 1808, and soon after entirely disappeared. They gradually tended westward, and now for many years none are seen east of the great rivers of the West."

Though huge and apparently clumsy, the Bison is exceedingly playful and frolicsome, gambolling as we see domestic cattle do.

Rev. J. G. Wood, 1885
Author

While I stand listening, there comes, borne upon the south wind, a faint tinkling note that thrills me more than all other sounds. It cannot be mistaken for any other, and I know the redwings are on the way. Whatever the time of year, there are joyful experiences in store for every rambler, but few that are more entrancing than to greet the crimson-shouldered blackbirds when they come in full force to the long-deserted meadows.

Charles C. Abbott, Late 1800s
Author

Many of these graves bore the appearance of being hastily made. Occasionally we passed one marked "killed by lightening," which was not surprising to us after having witnessed one of the most terrific thunder storms it had been our fortune to experience. This storm broke upon us after we had retired for the night. One after another, terrific peals of thunder rending the heavens in quick succession, roaring, rolling and crashing around, above and below, accompanied by blinding flashes of lightning, illuminating our wagons with the brightness of noonday, while the rain came beating down upon or wagon covers in great sheets. It was simply awful. Annie cried piteously to be "carried back home to Fazzer's house."

Phoebe Goodell Judson, 1853
Pioneer

On every side arose the unique forms of the Bad Lands, more wonderful and fantastic than at any other point before visited by me. Some portions look in the distance like cream-colored basaltic columns, others an amphitheater or the shape of arcs of a circle with a vast number of seats in many rows, one above the other; others resemble gothic temples, domes, towers, and fortresses. The west side of White Earth creek has much the appearance of a huge French palace, and as the early morning sun rests upon it every nook and corner seems lighted up with a strange wild beauty. The sides of these washed hills are worn into furrows, and every few feet there is a layer two to four feet in thickness, harder than the rest, which projects out, forming in many instances a sort of verandah.

Ferdinand V. Hayden, 1866
Geologist

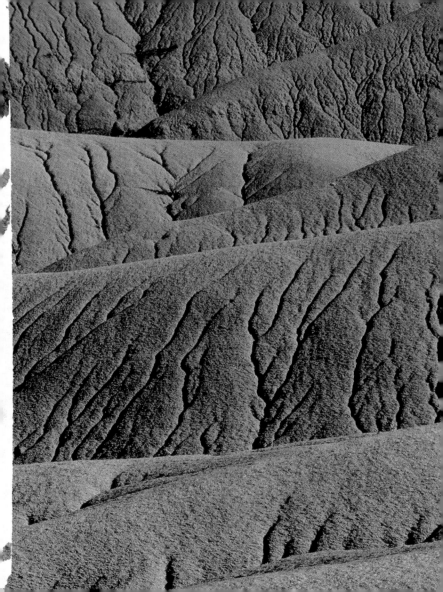

West and Mountains
Wilderness

WESTERN MOUNTAIN RANGES were unbelievable to expeditions sent to explore the new West. Perhaps it was the abruptness with which they rose, a mere fifteen miles from the plains to the crest, which was difficult to fathom.

Each naturalist venturing into these mountains, or through them en route to western destinations, was struck by the magnificence of the range. Hundreds of peaks crested above 12,000 feet. North America had never before presented explorers with such a challenge.

Deep within the earth at this Great Divide, two enormous blocks of super-heated terra firma jostle for position, their movement creating an upwelling of magma. In this area of thin earth and molten lava, mud bubbles and boils, steam rockets hundreds of feet into the air, and springs spew forth blistering hot water with the power of an awakened volcano.

The wilderness remembers a procession of pedestrians lightly stepping their way through this region, each marveling at such a wondrous place. More than 10,000 thermal features lurk under ponds, marshes, rocks, mud pits, and terraces here. This area so captivated those who first experienced its odd offerings, that nearly a century after it was first described, it was designated as the United State's first national park, Yellowstone. It was to become the cornerstone of a system to preserve the wilderness of North America, and a model for wilderness conservation worldwide.

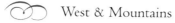

. . . . in the form of an immense fortification with turrets and rock-crowned battlements, and pine trees along the covered line relieved against a clear blue sky. . . appeared to be guarded by large terraced watch-towers.

Anonymous Dragoon Journal, 1835

The people there do not know what a canoe is; as there is no wood in all that vast extent of the country, for fuel they dry the dung of animals. There is the mountain the stone of which shines night and day, and that from that point you begin to notice a rise and fall of the tide.

Cree Slave, 1738
With French Explorer Pierre Gaultier

The road through this hilley Countrey is verry bad passing over hills & thro' Steep hollows, over falling timber &c. &c. continued on & passed Some most intolerable road on the Sides of the Steep Stoney mountains, which might be avoided by keeping up the Creek which is thickly covered with under groth & falling timber . . .

William Clark, 1805
Explorer

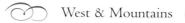

. . . remarkable white sandstone which is sufficiently soft to give way readily to the impression of water; two or three thin horizontal stratas of white freestone, on which the rains or water make no impression, lie imbeded in these clifts of soft stone near the upper part of them; the earth on the top of the Clifts is a dark rich loam, which forming a gradly ascending plain extends back from 1/2 mile to a mile where the hills commence and rise abruptly to a hight of about 300 feet more. The water in the course of time in decending from those hills and plains on either side of the river has trickled down the soft sand clifts and woarn it into a thousand grotesque figures, which with the help of a little immagination and an oblique view, at a distance are made to represent eligant ranges of lofty freestone buildings, having their parapets well stocked with statuary; collumns of various sculpture both grooved and plain, are also seen supporting long galleries in front of those buildings; in other places on a much nearer approach and with the help of less immagination we see the remains or ruins of eligant buildings; some collumns standing and almost entire with their pedestals and capitals; others retaining their pedestals but lying prostrate an broken.

Meriwether Lewis, 1805
Explorer

Desert Southwest
Wilderness

GEOLOGY . . . rocks and stuff. The American desert southwest is living geology. One can't wander through, between, and under its monoliths and mesas without being absolutely overwhelmed by the living presence of rock. Walls of it. Vertical plains that seem to defy mortal imagination.

Perhaps it is just such a thing that draws, and has always drawn, the human spirit to the desert southwest. There is little fluff about the landscape. Walls of sandstone are bare, crisp in line and rich in hue. And then there is the sky.

It is the sky that embraces the eternity of change here. Sky. Wind and air. They are the dance partners in this stony world.

A crack in the sandstone allows the wind to enter. Grain by exacting grain, the wind—now a sculptress—forms gentle, sinuous, curvaceous bends in eons-old layers of stone. This is an evolving landscape, a sculpture in progress. It is here that the union of wind and stone manifests itself.

The explorers who first traveled this landscape were totally entranced by this vast and beautiful, yet hostile environment. Their writings reflect the hold this rugged, yet rich land had upon them. Their willingness to leave behind any amount of comfort to walk or ride horseback through hundreds of miles of its rock, sand, sky, and wind proves that connection.

It takes patience to know such a place—and many returned again and again in search of an intimate knowledge of the land.

Since this is a hill country one expects to find springs; but not to depend on them; for when found they are often brackish and unwholesome, or maddening, slow dribbles in a thirsty soil. Here you find the hot sink of Death Valley, or high rolling districts where the air has always a tang of frost. Here are the long heavy winds and breathless calms on the tilted mesas where dust devils dance, whirling up into a wide, pale sky. Here you have no rain when all the earth cries for it, or quick downpours called cloudbursts for violence. A land of lost rivers, with little in it to love; yet a land that once visited must be come back to inevitably. If it were not so there would be little told of it.

Mary Austin, 1903
Author

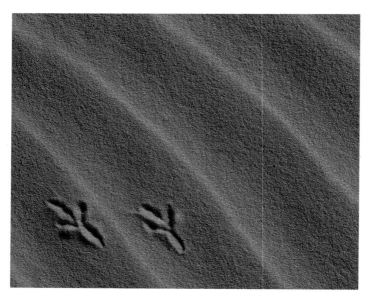

In all the vast space beneath and around us there is very little upon which the mind can linger restfully. It is completely filled with objects of gigantic size and amazing form, and as the mind wanders over them it is hopelessly bewildered and lost. It is useless to select special points of contemplation. The instant the attention lays hold of them it is drawn to something else, and if it seeks to recur to them it cannot find them. Everything is superlative, transcending the power of the intelligence to comprehend it. There is no central point or object around which the other elements are grouped and to which they are tributary. The grandest objects are merged in a congregation of others equal grand. Hundreds of these mighty structures, miles in length, and thousands of feet in height, rear their majestic heads out of the abyss, displaying their richly-molded plinths and friezes, thrusting out their gables, wing-halls, buttresses, and pilasters, and recessed with alcoves and panels. If any one of these stupendous creations had been planted upon the plains of central Europe it would have influenced the decorative art of Japan. Yet here they are all swallowed up in the confusion of multitude. It is not alone the magnitude of the individual objects that makes this spectacle so portentous, but it is still more the extravagant profusion with which they are arrayed along the whole visible extent of the broad chasm.

Clarence Dutton, 1882
U.S. Geological Surveyor

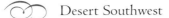

The glory of all this rock work is seen in the Pink Cliffs. . . The resemblances to strict architectural forms are often startling. The upper tier of the vast amphitheatre is one mighty colonnade. Standing obelisks, prostrate columns, shattered capitals, panels, niches, buttresses, repetitions of symmetrical forms all bring vividly before the mind suggestions of the work of giant hands, a race of genii once rearing temples of rock, but now chained up in a spell of enchantment, while their structures are falling in ruins through centuries of decay.

Clarence Dutton, 1882
U.S. Geological Surveyor

There are thousands of red, white, purple and vermilion colored rocks, of all sizes, resembling sentinels on the walls of castles, monks and priests in their robes, attendants, cathedrals and congregations. There are deep caverns and rooms resembling ruins of prisons, castles, churches with their guarded walls, battlements, spires, and steeples, niches and recesses, presenting the wildest and most wonderful scene that the eye of man ever beheld, in fact it is one of the wonders of the world.

T.C. Bailey, 1876
U.S. Deputy Surveyor

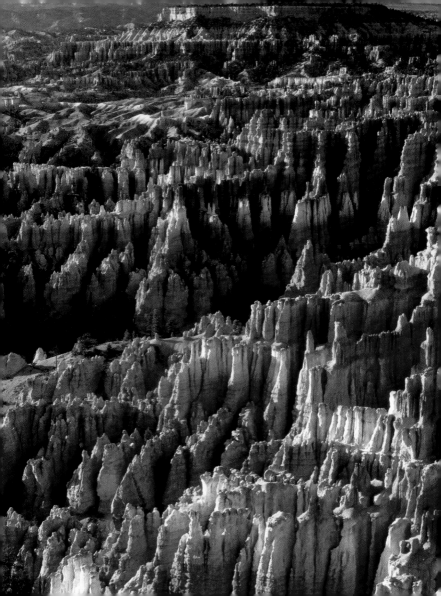

Pacific Northwest
Wilderness

COASTLINES wild and cold. The surging surface of a frigid sea. Ancient old-growth forests and alpine meadows. That is what separates North America's northwest coastal country from the remainder of the continent to the east. That and the densely forested, wet mountainsides and volcano foothills that fall to the sea.

Dampness is the one ubiquitous impression. For here, water is the one constant, the one ever-present factor of life to which every living and non-living force must adapt itself.

It quickly became clear to early explorers that all this water afforded a wealth of life. Seals and otters, bears and fish, waterfowl and the fruits of the forest helped to diminish the pressure of sheer survival in this wild land.

If water dominates the sensorial impression of the Pacific environment, then surely green overwhelms the visual. Yet it is again a vastly different world on the eastern side of these coastal mountains stretching along the Pacific Coast. Here the air is dry and dust rises. Days are hot and burning and turn with the fall of the sun to cold, crisp nights.

One cannot help but wonder, when watching an enormous high desert storm sweeping up the Clearwater River canyon, how consuming the complexity of this new North America must have appeared in the minds of these adventurers. Knowing they tread in a way, in a place, and in a time no other had and no others would again.

. . . *every where a thick forest of Pine, with scarcely a clear spot to be seen in the interior part; a high ridge of mountains extended themselves nearly in the direction of the coast. We observed great quantities of seals and Sea Otters; and often saw them rise from the bottom to devour large fish they brought up with them.*

. . . At 3 p.m. on the 29th our friendly breeze failed us, and not being far from the shore we anchored. . . the Land was every where covered with trees close down to the water side. A few fish were caught with hook and line and the jolly boat was given to me to try my luck in shooting. A few Sea gulls and a Cormorant was all I procurred. They made an escellent Pie and gave a good Supper to a Jovial Party.

Thomas Manby, 1792
Explorer

It is easier to feel than to realize, or in any way explain, Yosemite grandeur. The magnitudes of the rocks and trees and streams are so delicately harmonized they are mostly hidden. Sheer precipices three thousand feet high are fringed with tall trees growing close like grass on the brow of a lowland hill, and extending along the feet of these precipices a ribbon of meadow a mile wide and seven or eight long, that seems like a strip a farmer might mow in less than a day. Waterfalls, five hundred to one or two thousand feet high, are so subordinated to the mighty cliffs over which they pour that they seem like wisps of smoke, gentle as floating clouds, though their voices fill the valley and make the rocks tremble.

John Muir, 1911
Naturalist and Author

The river abounds with excellent salmon and most other river fish, and the woods with moose and deer, the skins of which were brought to us in great plenty. The banks produce a ground nut, which is an excellent substitute for bread and potatoes. We found oak, ash and walnut trees, and clear ground, which with little labor might be made fit to raise such seed crops as are necessary for the sustenance of inhabitants.

John Boit, 1791
Naval Explorer

. . . grizzly bears and wolves every night. The distant howl of a large wolf sounds much like the hooting of an owl, and the trinkling sound of snow-rills is scarcely heard. The forrest is still, except now and then the fall of a pine cone, sounding like a stone thrown. At dusk, the howl of approaching wolves is heard, coming up the Western dell; but the dogs take no notice of them, till they are quite near. They are accustomed to their howlings.

J. Goldsborough Bruff, 1850
Explorer

Far North
Wilderness

ALASKA IS MAGIC, and like no other place. Everything is larger, all consuming. And the insignificance of self is absolute. Grand things only. Grizzlies seem insignificant, moose seem insignificant, even a thousand sandhill cranes stretching from horizon to horizon seem insignificant. Lush, wet forests cover the land. Mountains rise from the sea and stretch for hundreds, or is it thousands, of miles. Volcanoes push their steamy heads above the surrounding glaciers. The tundra extends beyond vision, as well as imagination. And then, there's the ice—miles of ice reaching to the end of the earth.

Seasons sweep across the land and the land takes immediate notice. Sea ice forms, closing the avenues in which migrating beluga whales travel, but creating miles of pack ice for the white bear's travels. Icebergs calve off glaciers. Millions of birds make their annual migration. The tundra thaws, and in the short season, plants wake from their frozen depths, erupting in a sea of color across the vastness.

Explorers, early and late, came to the north and found themselves as much in love with the magic as with any concrete element. The reason for this lies in openness. Space, vastness.

Much of Alaska and the north remains untouched. There is no need to wonder what the land looked like before native people crossed the Bering land bridge, let alone what the first explorers saw. Stand here, now, and see it in its virgin, pristine state, with sandhill cranes possessing the sky, their voices echoing their ancestors' of ages past.

We were in the midst of strange scenes, hard to render in words, the miles upon miles of moraines upon either hand, gray, loosely piled, scooped, plowed, channeled, sifted, from 50 to 200 feet high; the sparkling sea water dotted with blue bergs and loose drift ice, the towering masses of almost naked rock, smoothed, carved, rounded, granite-ribbed and snow-crowned that looked down upon us from both sides of the inlet, an the cleft, toppling, staggering front of the great glacier in its terrible labor throes stretching before us from shore to shore.

We saw the world-shaping forces at work; we scrambled over plains they had built but yesterday. We saw them transport enormous rocks, and tons on tons of soil and debris from the distant mountains; we saw the remains of extensive forests they had engulfed probably within the century, an were now uncovering again; we saw their turbid rushing streams loaded newly ground rocks and soil-making material; we saw the beginnings of vegetation in the tracks of the retreating glacier; our dredges brought up the first forms of sea life along the shore; we witnessed the formation of the low mound and ridges and bowl-shaped depressions that so often diversify our landscapes—all the while with muffled thunder of the falling bergs in our ears.

John Burroughs, 1901
Naturalist and Author

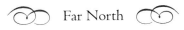
One and a half miles further brought us to a water-shed between the Tanana and Copper, where for the first time, was sighted the long sought Tanana waters. . . From this, the most grateful sight it has ever been my fortune to witness was presented. . . The views in advance and rear were both grand; the former showed the extensive Tanana Valley with numerous lakes, and the low unbroken range of mountains between the Tanana and Yukon Rivers. On this pass, with both white and yellow buttercups around me and snow within a few feet, I sat proud of the grand sight which no visitor save an Atnatana or Tananatana had ever seen. Fatigue and hunger were for the time forgotten in the great joy at finding our greatest obstacles overcome. As many as twenty lakes were visible, some of which were north of the Tanana, more than 20 miles away.

Lieutenant Henry Tureman Allen, 1885
U.S. Army Officer

Now is the moment to witness the display of the Eagle's powers. He glides through the air like a falling star; and, like a flash of lightening comes upon the timorous quarry, which now, in agony and despair, seeks, by various manœuvers, to elude the grasp of his cruel talons. It mounts, doubles, and willingly would plunge into the stream, were it not prevented by the Eagle, which long possessed of the knowledge that by such a stratagem the Swan might escape him, forces it to remain in the air by attempting to strike it with his talons from beneath. The hope of escape is soon given up by the Swan. It has already become much weakened, and its strength fails at the sight of the courage and swiftness of its antagonist. Its last gasp is about the escape, when the ferocious Eagle strikes with his talons the under side of its wing, and with unresisted power forces the bird to fall in a slanting direction upon the nearest shore.

It is then, reader, that you may see the cruel spirit of this dreaded enemy of the feathered race, whilst, exulting over his prey, he for the first time breathes at ease. He presses down his powerful feet, and drives his sharp claws deeper than ever into the heart of the dying Swan. He shrieks with delight, as he feels the last convulsions of his prey, which has now sunk under his unceasing efforts to render death as painfully felt as it can possibly be. The female has watched every movement of her mate; and if she did not assist him in capturing the Swan, it was not from want of will, but merely that she felt full assurance that the power and courage of her lord were quite sufficient for the deed. She now sails to the spot where he eagerly awaits her, and when she has arrived, they together turn the breast of the luckless Swan upwards, and gorge themselves. . .

John James Audubon, Early 1800s
Ornithologist and Painter

The chain of mountains before mentioned is broke by a plain of a few leagues in extent, beyond which the sight was unlimited, so that there is either a level Country or water behind it. . . . the mountains are wholly covered with snow, from the highest summits down to the sea-coast; some few places excepted, where we could perceive trees.

Captain James Cook, 1778
Explorer

NorthWord Press
5900 Green Oak Drive
Minnetonka, MN 55343
1-800-328-3895

Library of Congress Cataloging-in-Publication Data
Ellis, Gerry.
    Wilderness explored / photography by Gerry Ellis ; text by Karen Kane.
        p.   cm.
    ISBN 1-55971-712-2 (hc)
    1. Natural history--North America Pictorial works.   I. Kane, Karen.   II. Title.
QH102.E45   1999
508.7'022'2--dc21   99-30924

Printed in Singapore